PLEASE DON'T GO BEFORE I GET BETTER

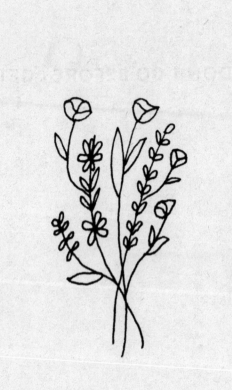

PLEASE DON'T GO BEFORE I GET BETTER

Madisen Kuhn

G

GALLERY BOOKS

New York   London   Toronto   Sydney   New Delhi

Gallery Books
An Imprint of Simon & Schuster, Inc.
1230 Avenue of the Americas
New York, NY 10020

First Gallery Books trade paperback edition May 2018

GALLERY BOOKS and colophon are registered trademarks of
Simon & Schuster, Inc.

For information about special discounts for bulk purchases,
please contact Simon & Schuster Special Sales at 1-866-506-1949
or business@simonandschuster.com.

The Simon & Schuster Speakers Bureau can bring authors to your
live event. For more information or to book an event, contact the
Simon & Schuster Speakers Bureau at 1-866-248-3049 or visit
our website at www.simonspeakers.com.

Interior design by Joy O'Meara
Illustrations by Leah Lu

Manufactured in the United States of America

20   19   18   17   16   15   14   13   12   11

Library of Congress Cataloging-in-Publication Data is available.

ISBN 978-1-5011-9681-2
ISBN 978-1-5011-9682-9 (ebook)

this is for anyone who aches to feel understood.

for anyone who is aching to find some sort of connection in a world full of missed ones. i hope that you find reassurance in these pages. that they validate your own journey and assure you that you are not alone. that is all i could ever ask for. that my words make you feel something. that you read what I've written while navigating the confusing and windy roads of existence and feel that your soul has been met with understanding and acceptance. you and i, we are linked in love and the energy that steadily courses through the universe. we are trying.

madison

PLEASE DON'T GO
BEFORE I GET

contents

contents

contents

PLEASE DON'T GO BEFORE I GET BETTER
PLEASE DON'T GO BEFORE I GET BETTER
PLEASE DON'T GO BEFORE I GET BETTER
PLEASE DON'T GO BEFORE I GET BETTER
PLEASE DON'T GO BEFORE I GET BETTER
PLEASE DON'T GO BEFORE I GET BETTER
PLEASE DON'T GO BEFORE I GET BETTER
PLEASE DON'T GO BEFORE I GET BETTER
PLEASE DON'T GO BEFORE I GET BETTER
PLEASE DON'T GO BEFORE I GET BETTER
PLEASE DON'T GO BEFORE I GET BETTER
PLEASE DON'T GO BEFORE I GET BETTER
PLEASE DON'T GO BEFORE I GET BETTER

rough draft

you make so much sense
amidst the tangled vines of
learning and unlearning
please don't go before i get better

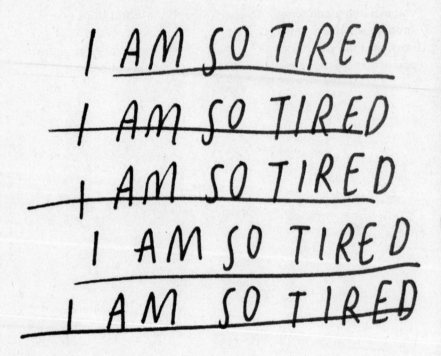

sleep talk

i want to keep falling asleep to your voice till the world stops existing. i wish i could dissolve up out of my body and take a photo from above of me lying here, arms outstretched and duvet covering most of me except for a few strands of hair peeking out because then you could see how tired i am, i am so tired.

sunday, april 23rd

the panic begins at night
and it follows me through
the day,
anchors me to my bedroom
floor when everyone begins to
shut their doors and turn out their
lights

my ceiling doesn't look like
a galaxy, or even just a
ceiling, it feels like a hand
lowering
itself, slowly,
until i'm stuck beneath fingernails

i change my sheets, bathe my dog,
it lingers inside my throat
my twin mattress feels like i'm
drowning in a bathtub

there are tan lines on my
shoulders where your arms should be

in my house, i'm not alone,
but when the moon is in the sky,
and my friends are in their beds,
and these incessant thoughts
are in my head,

i might as well be

landmark

nineteen has taught me a lot about being alone. i've listened to chvrches a lot these past few months. a lot when i've been alone— in my room, on the bus, in my car. tonight, i knew i'd be by myself since i was getting there late and it's nearly impossible to find friends in dead zone music festivals. i don't like being alone in public for the most part. it makes me nervous. but tonight was something i really needed. i let go of all my anxious thoughts and allowed myself to be in the moment. i danced in my overalls and chucks, surrounded by strangers who i knew didn't care how ridiculous i probably looked (white girl cursed with no rhythm).

i was completely alone, surrounded by hundreds of people, consumed by music that i love, and it was so full. they played "tether," which is a song i've been dying to hear live for a while now. it was amazing. i couldn't stop thinking about how happy i was. a girl i didn't know, whose friend was in a bear suit, came up and hugged me because she was "just so excited." (thought this random pda was super cute even though it was probably drug- or alcohol-induced. whatev.)

it was a magic hour that made me feel so alive. it was a moment i didn't mind being alone in.

i'm learning how to spend this time alone with myself. you begin to notice these moments: in your room, in the car, at the mall. grocery shopping, getting your cracked phone screen fixed, driving home for the weekend. it's scary and new and weird. it can be hard, and it has been for me. i'd never really thought about how lonely these years could be. of course i'm surrounding myself with friends that i adore, but time spent alone is unavoidable. and being alone isn't necessarily bad. it's just a part of life. someone can't always be there with you at the doctor's office or in the bookstore line. i'm getting to know myself very well in these moments in time where the only company i have is myself.

i needed tonight. i needed to let go and not care who was looking. i needed to sing and jump and be happy. it's amazing how music can do that: make life feel so much more real.

magnets

i'm in a constant battle with reality and pretend
with who i am, who i want to be,
and who i wish i could be

with picking up the pieces, painting portraits of some-
thing strong, something whole,
something to be proud of
and shattering crystal vases on wooden floors

while smiling, without blinking
with seeing just how far i can run away from myself
without forgetting myself

i lie in my bed, and i sip my tea
and it feels like the rain outside is going to
swallow me whole

and i'm happy
and i'm sad
and i'm panicked
and i'm trapped
and i'm everything
and i'm scared

and the sky is dark
blue and the night is
so dizzy

     and so am i
and i've forgotten how to exist

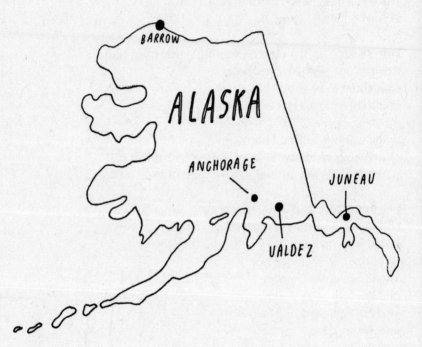

alaska

you are not a hospital room
you don't have to keep everything
pure-white and sterile

you are ugly red clay on the walls
covering up your bruises with
pink cotton-candy fluff and
bright yellow smiley-face stickers
that you saved from first grade
living out of your car
and calling it a slumber party; sleep-away camp
far away from the monsters beneath your bed

you don't have to paint your cheeks
with roses, leaving out parts of you like
a mad libs story we played to pass the time
on long car rides to the coast

we can sit in silence
while the world around us buzzes
with all its uncertain chaos and
my soul will find yours
in the space that rests above
this mess of existing

when i want to be on your team

1. when we pass our exit in the dark
2. in a well-lit gas station parking lot three miles away from home
3. when you spend too much money on the claw machine
4. at midnight, fifteen people ahead of us in the walmart checkout line
5. my driveway, sitting in silence with the windows fogging up
6. twin beds
7. when you swear, but take it back
8. when i don't take my own advice
9. freezing cold, looking at the sky, listening to someone talk about how god created the universe just to give us an existential crisis
10. morning breath
11. when you want to dance in front of the mexican restaurant
12. oversleeping
13. getting ready in ten minutes to catch the bus
14. shitty putt-putt on a monday evening
15. walking around old navy and realizing there is nothing for us here
16. a brown paper bag from rite aid
17. when you remind me to wash my hands
18. when my shirt doesn't match my shorts
19. sitting on a crowded sidewalk and remembering how to breathe
20. when i don't know how. when it's easy. when it's hard. when you need me to be. always.

irises

i'm not sure how artists have the patience
to sculpt marble slabs into gods
or why they feel it's worth their time

but i do know that
the nights i stay up until 3 a.m. are usually the worst
and the mornings i wake up at 8 a.m. are usually the
best

and that it's worth the money to buy a decent mattress
instead of losing sleep on fiscal responsibility
and i feel grown-up having wrapping paper in my closet
and extra birthday cards in my desk

and i might always be crazy
always holding on to pieces of the past
tacking them to my bedroom walls
and pretending it's okay that i still think about it all

but i won't forget that some people are brave enough
to put on big white suits and fishbowl helmets and leave
their families to go walk on the moon
or that i flew on a plane by myself even though i was
absolutely petrified of being alone in the sky
or that spring exists,
and that winter cannot, and will not, last forever

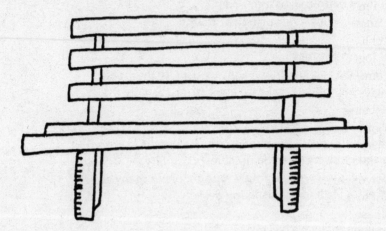

astronomy club

i have a crush on a boy
but i'm afraid of hurting his feelings
because ever since late january
i feel like i don't really have any myself
just logic to judge
no emotions to indicate
he says he needs to be careful with his heart
and being cautious may pay off in the end
you may end up with less
fingerprints and teeth marks on your ribs
but right now i have no interest
in anyone who doesn't
want to let feeling consume them
to chase their impulses
into the dark, by the pond behind my house
maybe you should have kissed me

people over places

i'm realizing over and over again that life is about the people you
share it with. the kind of people you just feel good around. the kind
who make you feel whole.

new york by itself is just another city.

i know if i packed up all my things and cozied up in a tiny studio
apartment in manhattan and kept to myself, it wouldn't be enough.
the city makes me feel so alive, but in huge part because of who i'm
with when i'm there. it's the people you get to navigate the subway
with, eat brunch with, and browse overpriced ceramic and home
goods stores with that make it so special.

i'll keep coming back again and again, not just for the beautiful
cityscapes, diversity, and endless possibilities, but especially for all
the beautiful people i love who have found a home there.

new york city, forever in my heart.

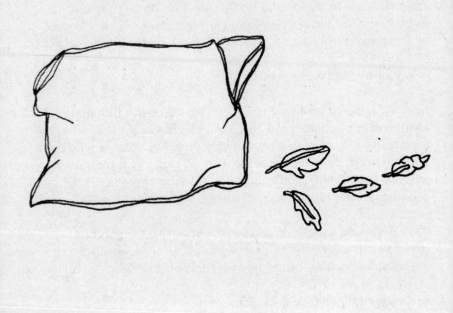

half-awake

i always regret the nights i stay awake
for no reason at all
except to trace and retrace every fear
that lies awake on my chest
the evening grows closer to the sun
and more unproductive
c h o p p e d
into little bits where the light creeps in
a hazy glow, lost memories that are insignificant
and not much of a loss
down feathers scattered across an orange sunrise
and pillows piled on top of piercing silence
all i wish
is to be asleep
tucked into a dreamland
where nothing can excite me

you used to make me
feel like there were magnets
inside my cheeks and behind
your lips.

i was happy

this was my life, and i was happy. i was happy with the security, with the consistency, with the repetitiveness of you and me. i was happy lying in your bed for hours. i was happy listening to you talk to your dog in the most ridiculous baby voice i'd ever heard. i was happy brushing my teeth with you. i was happy always holding your hand. i was happy driving hours to see you. i was happy listening to you sing, and i missed it when your voice began to fade. i missed it when you stopped kissing me like you used to. you used to make me feel like there were magnets inside my cheeks and behind your lips. you kissed me on the sidewalk, across the table in chinatown, in front of strangers. at first it made me shy, the way you didn't care about where we were or who was watching.

> you couldn't stop,
> and then you did.

you stopped doing a lot of things. i watched you slowly pale into something you didn't like. you were so consumed by so many things, it felt like a chore to be consumed by me. and it was fair. and i understood. and i didn't want to anchor you to something when you already felt like you were drowning. i guess sometimes we only know how to be partial versions of ourselves.

we sat in my car in your high school parking lot, ending things the same way we began them. i didn't really cry until the end, moments before we both drove away. i sobbed and tried to catch my breath in between words that felt so small and so helpless and so desperate. i wasn't ready to let go of you.

i mostly laughed because i kept looking at you and i couldn't believe how much i loved you. how much i knew i'd always love you. i laughed because i was staring at my best friend, a person who held so many pieces of me, but it felt like i was looking at you through solid glass. like you were right there, but i couldn't reach you. it wasn't funny, really. really, what it was—the laughter—was a feeling that was so strong that it bloomed inside my stomach and forced its way out of my throat, like a shaken-up can of diet coke. i felt crazy. i felt alive.

at first i coped by thinking this was temporary.
us,
        apart.

but as time went on, i realized that hopeful feeling was just that: a feeling. and feelings keep you up at night, and they make you feel sick when you're perfectly healthy, and they lie. i didn't want to convince myself of a false truth just to feel okay.

so i flirted with the idea of kissing a man with a mustache who was even older than you, and then i snapped back into the reality of how dumb of an idea that was. but it excited me. the thought of kissing someone else excited me, and i didn't feel guilty about it. i kissed other boys in my head; i held their hands and bit their lips and laughed. i wanted to feel more, but in different ways than before.

i wanted to be nineteen. i wanted to be reckless.
i wanted to not care. i wanted to be more like you.

at three in the morning, i thought about the possibility of you twirling another girl's hair between your fingers, lying in the glow and shadows of streetlamps that line the sidewalks of a city you helped me fall in love with, and i didn't know why, no clue, but i felt okay.

i was happy. i was happy drawing circles on your back and dragging my nails down your tattooed arms. i was happy trying new things with you, things you knew i'd like even though i was stubborn, like lemon ricotta pancakes. i swear you always knew me better than i knew myself. you saw me in ways i didn't know how to see myself yet. i was happy listening to you snore while i lay wide awake. i was happy hearing you talk about things that mattered to you, and realizing they mattered to me, too.

and maybe i'll be happy letting myself tumble through the crashing waves, getting sand in my swimsuit bottoms and salt water up my nose, spinning around, and, despite it all, running back towards the ocean again. maybe i'll be happy in blue eyeliner and ripped tights.

there are two lies that are very easy to let myself believe:

1. my heart is irreparable
2. my heart is indestructible

i refuse to be fooled by either.

CARESSING THE MEMORIES OF A GHOST

nosferatu

i was sixteen, you were pretending
young and lonely, someone else
my imaginary friend,
who was never really a friend

deep in the shadows, you lurk,
a memory that won't repress,
you were a distraction
from my mess of a reality, a place
to freely feel, although it was ugly

a mess
apart from
a mess

one that was okay because
it didn't really exist,
a black-and-white silent film,
spinning on the screen and then forgotten,
i could turn it off and it would
be gone, you would be gone, you are gone

but you were never really there,
and i lie here motionless
caressing the memories of a ghost

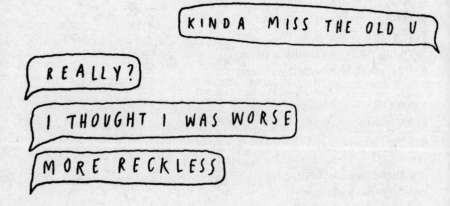

beginnings always seem better through rose-tinted sunnies

something i've recently discovered about myself (thanks to some external criticism) is that i am, in some twisted way, addicted to hurting. for whatever reason, i continuously search for things to hurt me. i expect the people i care about to always have some secret, cynical second layer of being hiding beneath their skin; a layer that does not care about me. i ask questions even though i know the answers will do nothing but get stuck in my head and come up again and again as they please, sharpened and ready to kill whatever sense of confidence or security i'm holding on to at any given moment.

i connected my external hard drive to my current laptop. i did this because my laptop has been saying the startup disk is full and i have no idea why, so i was just going to clear it and start fresh. funny, i wanted a clean slate, but instead i got stuck in the trenches of a year-old iphoto library, looking at old screenshots from the beginning stages of a relationship that's currently wrapped up in a nostalgic little coffin.

you said:
> *i still think you're incredible*
> *come live with me*
> *forever*
> *please*
> *and let's just hug*
> *can i call you today or tomorrow*
> *do you miss me*

i read these texts from last october and told you:
> *kinda miss the old u*

to which you replied:
>   *really?*
>   *i thought i was worse*
>   *more reckless*

so i clarified:
>   *i mean the way you texted me*
>   *nice being told ur incredible u know*

and you said:
>   *i was saying that and also being terrible tho*

and you were right.

it's easy to look back and romanticize the bits of time when you were first getting to know someone. both of you were looking at each other the same way you have to look at the sun when it's in the middle of the sky; squinting because it's so bright. then once you get to know them deeply, you look at them the same way you look at the moon—you can stare at it for hours, mesmerized by its glow, and not say a word. in the beginning, you see an incomplete version of someone. as time goes on, you begin to see someone fully, and you no longer have to wear your polarized ray-bans, and somehow that makes it feel less significant, when really, it's the opposite, because now, it's real.

i have to remind myself that:

1. whenever he wakes up in a half-asleep daze, he always reaches for me, or kisses me, or rubs his thumb on the back of my hand, and pulls me closer
2. sitting in the passenger seat as I drove around aimlessly for an hour and a half on new year's eve because i was upset and didn't want to be at home, he told me in the 7-eleven parking lot while i cried at 1 a.m., "i think you're being too hard on yourself"
3. spending hours caring for my dog when she was ill

4. buying last-minute christmas gifts the day before christmas eve and wrapping an impossible-to-wrap basketball for my brother
5. encouraging me to brush my teeth after i've already gotten in bed despite my whiny protests
6. not taking my bullshit
7. listening to 2009 alternative rock in his car with a box of krispy kreme doughnuts in my lap
8. meaning everything he says

—is better than any mushy text message from when he barely knew me.

(i guess in some way we're always romanticizing something. in my attempt to explain that the romanticizing that happens in the beginning stages of relationships pales in comparison to the vulnerability, authenticity, and selflessness of deeper human connection, i romanticized very normal scenarios and may have painted them to be more significant than they probably were.)

sometimes, i look at him and it feels like he's the only person i ever want to know. other times, i look at him and think about what a beautiful first love he was, and how i'll always remember the special space in time we shared, but in my bones i feel there is more for me to feel elsewhere. maybe that's just me coping.

things with us aren't perfect, which i'd say should be expected of any relationship. and maybe things with us aren't even what they're supposed to be, but i'm nineteen, and i've never kissed anyone else, and i'm not sure how i'm supposed to know what is and what is not worth fighting for. all i know is that i care for him, very much.

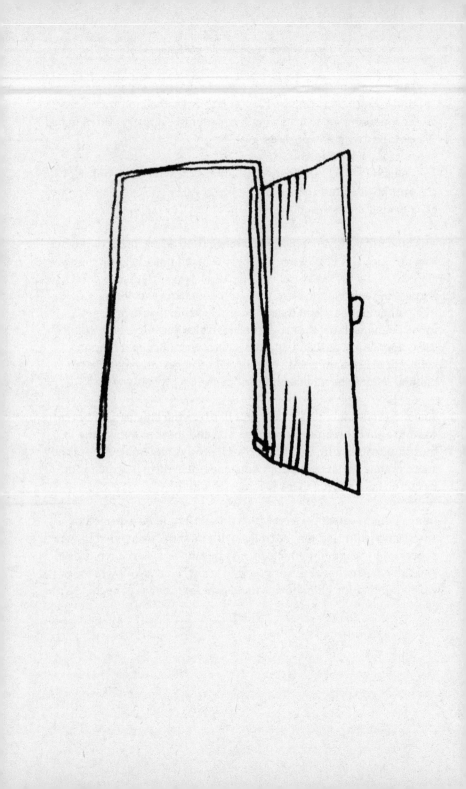

she would want you to

this morning, i stood in a doorway and cried because leaving is hard. i drove an hour home and listened to bear's den on repeat.

this afternoon, i drank hot apple cider and walked around old towne in a dress and couldn't believe how nice it felt outside in december. i picked up a newspaper and did the crossword and sudoku. i felt like my grandmother.

this evening, i cleaned out my dresser drawers and filled up an entire trash bag with clutter. i ate chinese takeout and played monopoly with my dad and laughed while watching angel attack the new squeaky unicorn toy i bought her.

tonight, i'm thinking about the beauty of embracing life's chaos with knowing that we can't choose a lot of things, but we can choose to be good people. we can choose to love without ulterior motives, and to be stronger than our emotions make us feel, and to always keep spinning forward. it's all okay, it always will be.

beautiful alone

i started seeing the stars brighter when you left. started seeing myself
brighter. before, all i could see was

y o u.

i could barely see myself. my soul was starving and my heart worn,
falling into bed every night without taking time to change the sheets.
i hate to admit it, but i think i forgot how to be myself once i had you.
maybe it was the timing, and maybe i was just divided—my feet in
two doorways, leaving one place and entering another. i was stuck
in the hallway with starch-white walls and no light. and i ignored
it because i could, because i had you to distract me. but now i can't
avoid it. i look at my life now and see it as cold, hard clay, aching
for my hands to turn it into something beautiful, something with
meaning. everything is falling, and i'm surrounded by empty water,
but i feel like i'm being reborn. i forgot how to look at the world
through my rose-colored glasses; lost them in my mother's house
and settled for grey. that isn't me. maybe i was too crowded by
rosebushes smothering me from seeing any sort of sunlight, but now
the soil is clear and all i can do is let the sun touch me until i turn into
something just as beautiful alone.

my first kiss

i had a temperature of one hundred point five and i'd puked on the train on the way to see him. it was the first time i'd ever been close to anyone, really close, so close it felt like my skin was on fire (but looking back, maybe that was just the fever). he held me on his mom's blue couch; his dog (who was named after a rapper and smelled like pumpkin because he'd just returned from the groomer's) lay at our feet. i felt nervous, excited, dizzy. we watched the office. he gave me tylenol. i ate chicken noodle soup on his floor. we sat back to back and i laughed at how ridiculous we already were together; how comfortable i already felt with him. i was always comfortable with him. there was silence, but not the type that felt echo-y. it was cliché and it wasn't. we laid on his bed and watched television until the sun set; pushed his curtains aside and looked at the moon like we did in his car on the first night we met. he said the moonlight was painting me. dragging fingers across my skin, he labeled my bones. i remember him kissing my face so many times i was afraid he'd accidentally miss and kiss my lips and the thing i'd been saving for eighteen years would suddenly be gone. but then hours later, after hours and hours of learning the art of being close, i kissed him. and i've kissed no one else since.

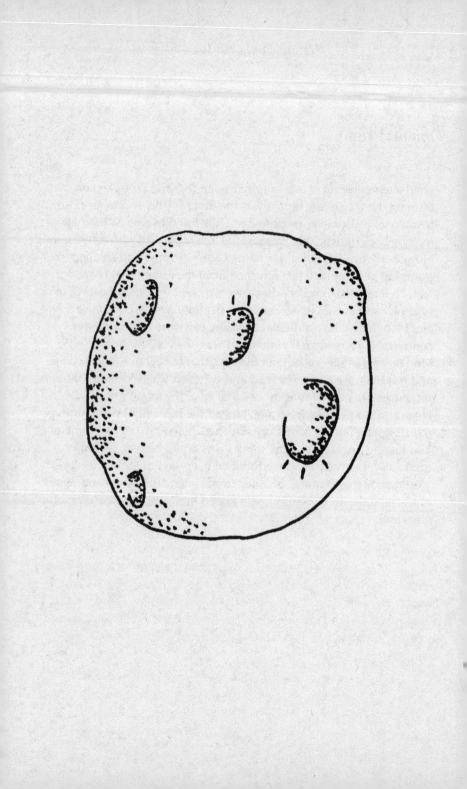

rest

i wrote about a boy the night we met, glasses and a polka-dot shirt i never thought would leave the stars and trees of that early morning in august. it felt like a lunar eclipse, a moment where i stood with my face up to the sky, straight on and uninhibited, but never expecting the moment to stay. moments like these come and go, and are accepted as fleeting; special dates to mark on the calendar, not penciled in on every square. i believed that he was fleeting. that my moons would always be grey. yet, i kept writing about him, a crimson moon with a recurring theme of crimson feeling—full of passion, anger, pain. i felt more inclined to write about him when my skin would crawl, rather than when my heart would flutter. maybe it was because our hearts were always beating, but never in time with one another. i was afraid that my poems would become gravestones, filling a cemetery of our almost love, hurtful reminders of what i'd never fully had until,

now

my heartstrings are completely entangled with his, a mess of indistinguishable shades of lavender that hum melodies of both obsession and safety. when i left him in those early august hours, my dreams of him faded the next morning. they turned to dust as soon as the sun touched the horizon, for four hundred and seventy-two days. i thought i'd lost something i'd never get back. i did. i watched our mercurial infatuation die, and from its ashes rose a love like nothing i'd ever known. and now my dreams of him stretch into the abyss of time, eager and familiar, as if there's only ever been crimson moons hanging in the sky.

I AM A
MESS OF
CONTENTMENT
AND WONDER

p.s.

i am overwhelmingly in love and it is the most peaceful yet
exhilarating feeling in the entire world. i feel like rain, a tornado, and
the sun peeking out from behind the clouds after a violent storm,
all at the same time. i am a mess of contentment and wonder.
he is all i've ever wanted.

june

an afternoon accompanied by
rushing water and rustling trees,
the scent of a spruce candle burning,
i recalled that fire is often described as
something unapologetic,
a force that burns through forests
with resilience, and power, and no inclination to look
back; this is something i've spent my whole life trying
to be

but i saw myself in the flame of a candle
burning in a different light,
i saw something soft, and warm, and calm
something reborn, consumed
whipping itself back and forth as the wind blows it,
dancing from side to side like an eager child
it makes no effort to keep still
it accepts the movement, the wind, the chaos
and as it lets itself go,
as the wax melts down
slowly
      slowly
           slowly
it glows.

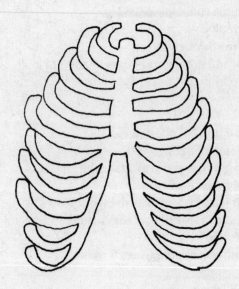

forget-me-not

"you've changed."

digs itself between your ribs
gripped by the hands of someone
who had already painted their portrait of you
but then you came along and sprinkled
rose-colored glitter across your cheeks
dragged sky-blue painted fingertips
down the sides of your face
exhale deeply
dust off your hands
different looks like ghosts to some;
they don't see people as perennial flowers, ones that
bloom in the summer, but wither by winter
only to bud again as something new in the spring
they assume autumn's mess of orange and brown is the
end—
that things cannot be reborn
so clenched fists punch holes through canvas
leaving red-glittered knuckles and
spit that looks like teardrops
without considering that maybe blue
has always been your color

gap

lulls of silence—
wide-open meditative spaces
where everything is washed
and vacant,
stretching on into pale skies
in every direction,
void of anything
it is lonely, maddening,
a desert, my home
where i feel very small,
where there is nothing
to run towards—
they haunt me like shadows looming
on bedroom ceilings
above twin beds,
where i lie below, motionless
with a dream catcher
hanging on the wall above
my messy, braided hair and
chapped lips buried
into a pillow,
empty

the first year

we drove up the coast with the wind lapping our cheeks, violently whipping my hair into my mouth in that way that's both annoying and careless—you keep the windows down even though the wet strands repetitively collide with your eyelashes; you squint and laugh and show your teeth for bugs to get stuck in between.

i sat in the passenger seat for most of the trip, and when we switched in the afternoon, i had to pull over twice in south carolinian driveways because i felt like i couldn't breathe. he didn't ask me if i needed him to take over, didn't give me the out that i desperately wanted. because that was what i wanted, right? i was told that girls lie asleep on beds of thorns and only kisses make them feel alive. i was told that this is what i should dream of.

instead, he sat with me, patiently, and told me i was okay. i'd take a deep breath, sip the arizona sweet tea that he bought for me at 7-eleven, and back out of gravel roads, back onto the long stretch of highway ahead, and start again. and again. two hours in, with the windows back down—because i knew there was more air on earth than my lungs could ever hold—i listened to tori kelly's rendition of "baby, baby," and with the entire sun in my eyes, i thought, *this is what it's like to be okay.*

i don't know how this fell into my lap. this person who bugs me with too many questions and falls asleep twenty minutes into movies and forgets to turn my headlights on when he drives my car.

this person who introduced me to falafel, and philadelphia, and nickel creek. this person who pushes me and grows with me and doesn't let me settle or scrape by because he sees more in me than i see in myself.

most of the time it makes me want to scream, because he won't let me hide away in my knitted blankets and fuzzy socks, believing i can be perfectly happy with mediocrity and binge-watching stranger things in the dark. but then i look at him, with his ginormous brown eyes that never shut, always ready to let himself be consumed by everything around him, and realize that neither of us was ever meant for ordinary.

philadelphia

it's fascinating to observe how different surroundings affect my spirit. christopher and i are staying in a studio apartment next to rittenhouse square. it's thoughtfully decorated and minimalistic, with artwork on the walls and mixed patterns. mrs. meyer's basil-scented hand soap in the bathroom, records on the bookshelf, and hardwood floors. walking on the sidewalks of buzzing streets with the sun beating down on my face—through a park crowded by people on benches, sitting in the grass, a group of moms with their toddlers on colorful duvets, dogs lying in the shade, both businessmen and women in spandex meeting friends for lunch. being alone—it makes me feel surrounded and empowered. i feel inspired and capable of achieving greater things than what i am currently experiencing. being here provokes an eagerness to inspect all the areas of life in which i am lacking. to tear down the wallpaper and roll on fresh paint. right now, i feel i am someone who is cold, insecure, nervous, idle. i am not the person i dream of being. i want to be warm and joyful, like i used to be before i decided i was too fucked up. i crave harmony in my relationships—i want to be better at considering others' pain, and understanding their points of view without making snap judgments. i want to be patient. i want to be the free spirit i know that i am, not limited by my anxiety or depression. i want to be independent, like i feel when i walk by myself in the city. i want to look at other girls and see loveliness rather than competition. i want to be so content with who i am that i forget to consider myself at all—instead, i just exist. i want to be self-aware, to know exactly what i want and need, and to go after it without hesitation. i want to chase the life i envision for myself. this is a start.

disciples

the only thing that inspired me today
was washing my feet in the shower

i noticed it wasn't something i do very often
a task neglected by staring contests with productivity
i won't blink first
i won't slow down
it felt innocent, and intimate, and thoughtful
and so, so normal; normalcy that i craved
with burning water running down my back

i bought a couch for a dream
i'll be living in
one week from now
where every day will begin and end
with him

i'll remind us both to wash our feet

better times

too often we find ourselves either chasing the future or trapped in the past; grasping for moments that always feel just out of reach, or suffocating in memories that keep us from sleep—both preventing us from fully embracing the present. we get stuck on "the good ole days," convinced things will never be as good as they once were. we become ghosts living in places that don't exist yet, thinking happiness will only find us after we've achieved all the checks on our lives' to-do lists. once i graduate, i'll be happy; once i get a good job, i'll be happy; once i move to new york city, i'll be happy. we get so fixated on every level of consciousness that isn't embracing the current. but maybe it's time to stop letting our minds wander to places that are gone, or haven't arrived yet. maybe it's time to open the curtains and feel the sun on our skin and realize that existence is a series of nows. maybe it's time to start realizing that the best times aren't behind us, and better times aren't ahead of us—better times are here, and they're happening right now.

hurry up, we don't have time to worry

sitting on your best friend's couch at 11 p.m., slightly sunburnt with a hoarse voice, haven't had time to breathe since last tuesday, i am exhausted in the best way and eager, rather than terrified, to face it all again tomorrow.

as long as i don't stop living

the past several days have been spent in cars packed with all our possessions, driving from obligation to obligation. i used to be surrounded by silence and static. each day would blend with the ones before and after it—a repetitive song of waking up, feeling sad, and hoping tomorrow would be better. i used to like being alone because no one could ask how i was doing, but then i grew afraid of being alone because no one would be there to save me if i wasn't okay. i was sick without a fever to prove it. it's funny how quickly things can change. i can't remember the last time i sat still and knew i'd be sitting still for a while. i keep moving, with the same feelings in my chest, the only difference is i don't let them freeze my feet. i hated my therapist when she told me, "it'll never go away, but you can learn to live with it." i wanted it to vanish like a bad dream in morning sunlight—a dried-up worm on the sidewalk that quickly turns to dust. i tried hiding in my closet, tried medicine, tried jesus. i existed without ever really doing anything at all, until what i wanted was worth being afraid. now i ride on trains, fly in planes, and drive hours and hours with only the wind and my dog as my company. i scream and cry until my eyes are bloodshot and tired, but i do not look back. days are so crammed together that taking an hour to write a poem is like hastily pulling teeth. soon, we'll be moved into our apartment and i'll cook breakfast in the mornings and walk the dogs in the afternoon and read by the pool. i'll paint, practice piano, start going to therapy again. life will be just as full, but less frantic. sleeping on mattresses that aren't mine is fun for a little while, and much better than the days when i was afraid to leave my own bed, but i'm ready to slow down again, even if i have to convince myself that it's okay to not be moving at a million miles an hour. as long as i don't stop living.

a soft summer afternoon

i spent the day in the city,
we ate lunch a few blocks down from the ballpark
and smiled at the parking attendant
who has never forgotten our faces
ever since my dad accidentally tipped him fifty dollars
instead of five

the sun soaked up my energy
and painted my cheeks with sunburn
as i watched my favorite team win
in the twelfth inning

it's now ten o'clock
and my eyelids are ready to close
as the night closes in,
content with the day's content

how lovely it is,
to not be plagued with
pre-slumber dreams of
insufficiency

how lovely it is,
to fall asleep
knowing that you lived today

AND MY MUSES
HATED ME AND
I DIDN'T EVEN
HAVE TO TRY.

knots like pretzels

everything is in boxes
in my mother's house
in my father's house
in the back of my trunk
different things in each of them
books and vinyl
jesus, innocence, mirrors
paintings that my little brother and sister
made for me at school
and i can't find my journal in any of them
i didn't used to have to tie strings
around my pinkies
to remind myself to breathe in words
i used to write too much
with ink smears tattooed on the
side of my left hand
i carried it around
sucking on my fingers
tasting the poetry drip
from my mouth like sticky mango juice
and people read it
and my muses hated me
and i didn't even have to try

a sorry sort of snake

with skin of ivory
that blushes at the sight of sun
even when the clouds are out,
i turn into a silly shade of pink
with a heart that drops
falls down, down, down
into a rabbit hole
at the sight of anything
remotely shattering,
gasping at little cracks on the sidewalk
carefully tiptoeing around bumblebees
with lungs that fill with cotton
in fear of a hansel and gretel gingerbread house;
lead me to the witch
where i will cry and wonder,
"how did i get here?"
and forget about
all the gumdrops in my stomach
with poise that only lasts seconds
in the face of spiders,
they crawl into my mouth
kept there until given the chance to spit
them back into your face
i will hold my breath
and picture fields of lavender
where a tanned girl spins carelessly
until my tissue-paper limbs
learn how to hold me up

slamming doors

on days like these, sunny and slow, i am supposed to be happy, but all i feel is emptiness and doubt. what if i always feel this way? maybe only some people have purpose or find purpose. how do i know if i am one of them?

anhedonia

the roads are wet
i don't know when it rained
maybe i'm not
a writer anymore
maybe i stopped
paying attention
maybe i left
behind all wonder
in my adolescence
maybe i forgot
how to find meaning
in ordinary things
flowery air
and lemonade
gingham dresses
and handwritten
letters covered in
glitter and cursive
maybe i need
to read more books
and take more walks
and spin more
beach house records
then, maybe then i'll find
stars in blue irises
and messy hair again

bathroom mirror pep talk

stay busy. don't let yourself freeze. move even if it feels like all your bones are broken and someone replaced your lungs with deflated balloons. those little voices in your head telling you that something is terribly wrong, that you are not okay, that there is no hope, that you should lay cement over your feet and accept defeat . . . they're lying. they are not you. maybe our brains aren't wired just right, but that's no excuse to abstain from life. if we aren't living, then what are we doing? it will pass, it always does.

a beautiful poem

80 degrees in the shade
with a breeze
by a pond with a fountain
sprinkling
overalls over calvin klein
underwear
on a thursday afternoon
in the summer
far away from an old home
closer to a new home
free,
       free,
              free

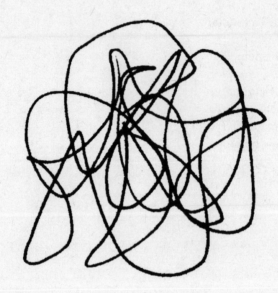

a shattered glass

you and i
broken windows
open only to embrace the
soft morning dirt
born with poison on our lips
devouring the universe
in small breaths
wondering why the days
feel so dizzy
again and again and again
there are no flowers here
there is nothing to help them grow

shower

this is
your open field
this is
where you lie on your back
on a fluffy, plaid duvet
eating strawberries
forgetting the sound of honking cars
and car alarms
this is your studio
replace the clay with bars of soap
paintbrushes with shampoo bottles
write your thoughts on fogged glass
lists of run-on sentences, scribbled
without inhibition
this is where the water runs off
your shoulders
this is where you reflect
it is not poetic
it is quiet, it is ordinary
knots of hair from gushing wind
smoothed over with aloe conditioner
everything is spinning, but here it slows
this is where you pause
this is where you breathe
this is where you begin again

i am clean,
i am clean,
i am clean.

pure

who would have thought i would become so obsessed with clean? not my mother, who'd nag me to pick up all the clothes scattered across my bedroom nearly every day of ninth grade. we rarely saw the floor. i'd sleep beneath books and laundry on my half-made bed. now i scrub dishes, scrub counters, scrub the floor at night because i can't stand the thought of a dirty kitchen—little cockroaches scurrying in and out of pots and pans. my home smells of lavender oil, a soft mist, air cleansed by a pink-glowing himalayan salt lamp and plants in the living room. now i put things away in drawers, close doors of rooms that are the slightest bit messy. now i straighten books on the coffee table, set the remotes parallel to one another, everything must be in place. now i floss, wash my face every night, stare in the mirror and repeat *i am clean, i am clean, i am clean.* now i burn my skin in the shower, inhale the steam until my breathing is slow and my sinuses are clear. *i am clean, i am clean, i am clean.* now i fold the laundry, stack our clothes into two piles, his and mine. i make our bed, i organize our shoes by the door, i kiss the man i love goodnight. *i am clean, i am clean, i am clean.* i know what my father must think, i know he loses sleep, i know there are holes in his tongue where his teeth have made a home. *i am clean, i am clean, i am clean.* i know he wishes i still went to church, wishes my boyfriend believed in a god, wishes i was clean. *i am clean, i am clean.*

october

will you still condemn me when
i am married to the man i welcome into my bed
because god is still not, and never was, a part of it?

subtlety

your eyes don't feel like daggers
they look like the reflection of a knife that is being
sharpened;
a promise

and i brace myself
every time you throw your hands in the air
and take it back the next morning

i bite my tongue so that when
you finally let go
i'll know the taste of blood;
it will not be a shock,
i will have seen it coming

you will not go out with thunder on your heels
you will leave in a whisper
or rather make me feel that it was my idea

you will give up before you go
a ghost of you making oatmeal in the kitchen
a heart already captivated by the enticement of
something new
something different
something that is not me

and i will have known the feeling
of you gone
long before
you've left

I FEEL LIKE I
AM WATCHING
EVERYONE ELSE
LIVE WHILE I WAIT
FOR MY TURN.

your twenties & stability: a paradox

i crave a home base so badly. somewhere that is somewhat permanent. i want a door to walk through, after being away for a while, where i can drop all my luggage and sigh because there is art on the walls, lights wrapped around the deck, a queen-size bed frame. it smells familiar, like lavender, like laundry. a place where i feel settled down enough to buy curtains instead of putting up flattened cardboard between the windows and the blinds. somewhere i have time to garden, or take painting classes, or go to therapy. a place with a café a few miles away that knows my order when i walk through the door, earl grey tea with honey and a blueberry scone. friends who come over on tuesday evenings and sit on my couch and eat the baked brie i've put out on the coffee table, laughing, the corners of their eyes crinkled, a fully contorted face that only appears when you're really, truly blissful. somewhere i can bring my neighbors muffins when they first move in and water their plants while they're away. our dogs will be friends and we can talk about politics between mailboxes. i want traditions, and family, and familiarity. where i am now is a place between places; traveling is a lifestyle, instead of a vacation; acting with the wisdom of a parent who doesn't want to buy their child expensive shoes because they know they'll grow out of them in just a few months. i feel like i am watching everyone else live while i wait for my turn.

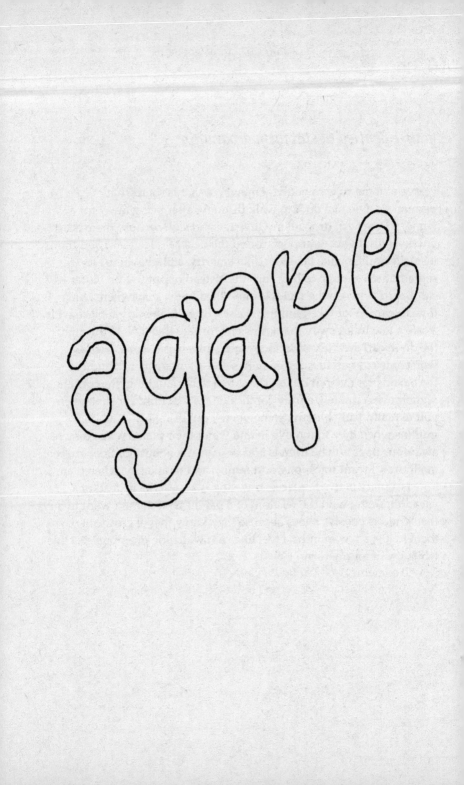

agape

they tell you to dispose of anyone who makes you feel
like
you aren't easy to love
but sometimes you aren't (easy to love)
some days you'll rock back and forth on the kitchen
floor
with terror dripping from your quivering lips
some days you'll need to be carried to the bathtub
while your mother pours water over your uncombed
hair
some days you will be a storm cloud, you will be a valley
you will be selfish, and cruel, and jealous
you will not be easy to love

but i will be here
to hold you in the middle of the parking lot
when it feels like the world is falling all around you
to pull you, kicking and screaming, out of the front door
so you can inhale fresh air and look up at blue skies and
be reminded that there are beautiful things
it will not be easy
it will take patience, and clenched fists, and slow breaths
it will sometimes feel unbearable (to love you)
you will feel like a burden; you will feel like you are not
enough
and i will love you
because you are more than the moments
when you cannot properly love me back

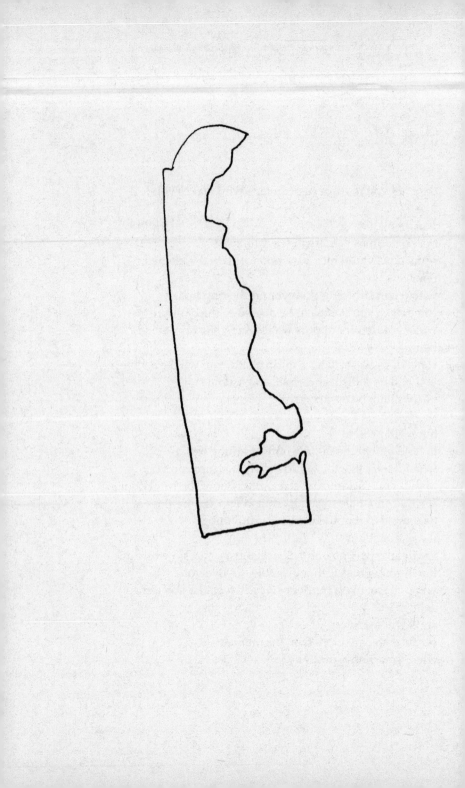

things that remind me of delaware

1. a travel-size spruce candle from p.f. candle co.
2. lavender essential oil
3. putting together furniture we shouldn't have bought
4. *depression cherry* by beach house
5. yellow gatorade
6. texas roadhouse
7. dairy queen onion rings
8. moldy flowers
9. my very first rice cooker
10. what it feels like to not have a father
11. reading *harry potter and the cursed child* by the pool
12. flattened cardboard boxes tucked inside bedroom blinds
13. learning how to be alone without letting it kill me
14. empty strip malls
15. noise complaints
16. talking him out of a tiny house right after graduation
17. *game of thrones*

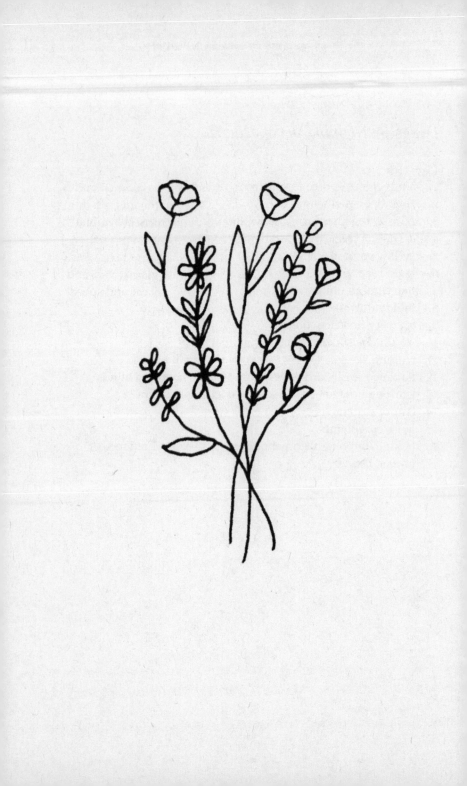

if i hadn't been moving so quickly

i forgot to buy flowers today. i bought a vase a few days ago and it's been sitting empty on our kitchen table. i went to the grocery store and rushed through the aisles, picking out sunscreen, provolone, tomato, a head of lettuce, and i forgot to buy flowers. i moved hastily to the self-checkout, threw it all in plastic bags, inches away from the florist, slipped out the automatic sliding glass doors, and walked briskly under the july sun, just to get in my car and speed through traffic lights. i forgot to buy flowers today.

emma

i love girls with inspired souls that radiate
while their heads are in the clouds,
spinning around and around and around and—
who has time to scan the crowds
to see if people are pleased?
am i amusing? do they like me?
she doesn't ask herself questions like these

she wears her thick and messy eyebrows
with pride and ease
rolls out of bed in her apartment
in the middle of a bustling city that is
full of possibilities, and no guarantees

but still, she chases it (it is anything, it is everything)
like an old lover who slipped away
when she was too young
to nurture a romance that, at the time,
felt much too cliché

and as each day passes by,
her dreams barrel into her like a dewy, ethereal mist
that illuminates her candid beauty

she laughs, and glows,
and dances until her feet are sore

and, oh god, she is free,
and she is everything
i hope to be

courage isn't fearless

this is not poetry. this is ripping your hair out on the highway, looking down at the clump of insanity in your hand, thinking *oh god what have i become*. these are cuts on the insides of your palms from clenching your fists so hard that the physical pain distracts you from the pain in your head. this is being alone. this is only having yourself. you are in a hotel parking lot in an unfamiliar town, and a man is tapping on your car window telling you he wants your dog while you sob on the phone to your father, telling him to not come get you because you do not want to be someone who always has to be saved. this is driving five minutes on the interstate while your heart races and your vision blurs, only to get back off and work up the courage to keep going all over again. this is yelling in your car alone, "i am strong. i am not my anxiety. i can do this." just so you can make it fourteen miles home. this is not poetry. this is self-neglect. this is avoiding therapy, avoiding medicine, avoiding growth, avoiding life. this is expecting people to always take care of you. this is asking for help before attempting to fix the problems for yourself. this is being a burden on the people you love. this is not being able to love as much as you want to because you are always putting your fears first. this is when you realize that you need to get your mental health under control before you destroy yourself completely. this is the moment that you tell yourself that you are in control. that you want to be so much more than who you are limiting yourself to being right now because you are not doing everything in your power to be better. this is knowing that even when you think you cannot, you can. this is your turning point. this is that scene in an '80s coming-of-age film where electronic music blares and someone sits on their front steps or on the hood of their car and realizes that they are capable of having everything they could ever possibly want, and their face is glowing and your heart feels warm just being there to watch it unfold. to see hope and crave it. this is when you look at yourself. really look at yourself. and decide that there is so much more that you will be.

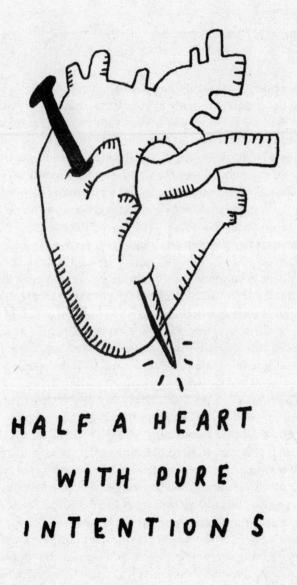

HALF A HEART
WITH PURE
INTENTIONS

i want you to cry, i want you to kiss me

i still remember the taste of nectarines
sweet and cold
held between sticky fingers
my abuelita would bring home bags of them
and i would plant the pits
in little plastic cups filled with dirt from the backyard
and place them on the windowsill above the sink

       i am half of a heart with pure intentions
       spinning in a world that is blurred
except for your face
       but you have kissed other girls
       and left trails of goose bumps across their
       breasts
       and they've fallen asleep in the same
       bed that is now mine

       i have loved other boys
       written poem upon poem about butterflies
       with their fingerprints
       on dusted and shimmery wings;
       i don't think of them anymore
all i see is you
       and all i wish
              is to be all you see, too

movement

i think we're soul mates,
and in another life,
we would meet
in the right place,
at the right time,
and grow old together.

bed of roses

i will never grow tired
of his arms around me
and listening to his slow breaths
while he sleeps
as i stay awake
to entertain the stars

happiness: you have to try

"happiness is all about perspective." it's what they all say, and they're all right. everything could be going wrong, but we have the power to choose to be optimistic and focus on the positives. little things. lavender epsom salt baths, sharing meals with people you love, and the way the sky changes colors when you're walking your dog in the evening. my heart is heavy, but at least i'm alive, at least it's beating. this is something that i'm terrible at. i have become such a pessimistic person and it's eating at my soul. this isn't who i want to be. i used to be able to see the good in everything, in everyone, and now my brain goes straight to the negatives and into a spiral of hopelessness. this has a lot to do with my anxiety and mood disorders (and having those extra obstacles is out of my control, it's not my fault. i have to remind myself of this), but it is still in my control to do the best i can to maintain my mental health and change my thought processes so i can be the happiest and greatest version of myself (this is also something i have to remind myself. my mental disorders are not an excuse to lie down and accept defeat). so i read this book that tells me to decatastrophize, and positive self-talk, and meditate, and i try. i found a therapist, i went to the gym with my boyfriend last week and felt sore for three days straight, and i'm doing my best to not let my fears keep me from living. today, as i was walking back from picking up a package at my apartment's leasing office, i thought about how perspective is #1, and environment feels a lot like #2. i lived in delaware for the summer, in an apartment way too big for the four of us, by the highway, surrounded by vacant shopping centers and not much else, and i was very sad for the majority of july and august. i wasn't happy there. i felt isolated and alone.

i could've been happy there. i could've changed my perspective and embraced the little things that made me happy, but i didn't. i could have done more, but i didn't. i didn't really try. but the thing is, if

you're in a place that you like, a place with good energy, it's a lot
easier to try. in delaware, we had a couch, a coffee table, a tv on tv
stand, a large dining table; here, we have a mattress, two nightstands,
a small kitchen table, and a projector. there is nothing on the walls,
not many personal touches, but it feels more like home here than
delaware ever did. it's just as hot here, but less sweltering, and the
leaves will change colors and become crunchy stepping-stones soon.
kids ride their scooters on the sidewalk and talk to me about my dogs.
our neighbors introduce themselves and smile instead of avoiding eye
contact. i feel less isolated, and more inclined to be a part of the space
around me.

i don't feel like time is frozen, like i'm missing out, i feel hopeful.
i feel happiness on the tip of my tongue. i feel like i can become the
person i've been talking about being for what feels like so long now.
and most of that is perspective, i've grown tired of always being so
tired and not doing anything about it. but it's also where i am, and i
am somewhere far away from where i grew up, far away from all my
friends and family, but i feel surrounded, and comfortable, and on the
verge of something wonderful.

naked

i've begun to use the shower curtain as a veil—the
flowing water to camouflage my tears—whenever i need
to cry
i am afraid to cry in front of him because he told me i
must cry to succeed; to collect the tears as fuel to hurl
myself into better things
he's told me i cannot simply cry as a gesture of defeat, that it makes
me weak, but sometimes i need to cry, not for any other purpose
except to let the hurt leave my body and whirl down the drain
hurt that says
you are your father's daughter
you are incapable of empathy
i tell him that it isn't true, and he tells me not to touch
him
i am too self-conscious to weep in front of a man whom
i share my bed with, a man who has seen all of me, so i
cry while the water burns me and he is fast asleep
i sing hideously along to "wolves" by phosphorescent
i cry and i am so glad he is unable to see me so
vulnerable, that he is not there to tell me to stop
i cry without inhibition and let snot drip over my lips
i cry because i cannot deny my humanness
i am not always strong
or empathetic, or right, or wrong
or capable
neither is he, neither is any of us;
every once in a while,
i wish he would join me.

sufficiency

when i feel like running away, i cannot find anywhere that i truly
want to disappear in. i consider every city i've considered before—
charlottesville, philadelphia, new york, dc—but they all feel
like wrinkled laundry. too familiar, lacking promise, excessively
expensive, uninspiring. they all have their own memories and
energies that prohibit them from truly being an emotional island;
a nonexistent dreamland, a new place where no one can reach me.
i can't seem to find the sense of escapism, isolation, excitement that my
heart desires. i crave a city where i can be no one, where i can blend
into the humming repetition of sidewalks and polluted air. i dream
of living alone in a studio apartment with hardwood floors and large
windows and white tile in an outdated bathroom. in this place—
which is most likely a state of mind, rather than something so tangible
as a location—i am alone, i am sufficient, i am free. i have no one
to get annoyed at for not doing the dishes. I cannot blame the high
electricity bill on my lover's obsession with being cold. there is no one
there to tell me that i must be more than i am. i am released from the
choking grasp of constantly seeking approval from those who i want
to love me without terms. i leave food out on the counter and throw
it away in the morning when i notice it's spoiled. i fall asleep in a
ball with the covers wrapped around me. i meet people who hold no
expectations for me—they simply take me as i am, as i pray that they
teach me the art of acceptance.

home

i haven't felt like i've had a home in quite some time. i've
always been split between
a few separate places.
there's hardly ever been any kind of consistency in my life, besides
my dog, and growing up has made it that much worse. i've moved
away from my parents' houses, i wouldn't call them homes, and this
place i've only known for less than six months feels warmer than
any house i grew up in. this bed, although smaller, sleeps easier. my
heart feels content in the dark and still when the morning light creeps
through my blinds. maybe it's because it's my space to create, space
that makes me feel safe. a safe haven filled with carnations in glass
vases and twinkly lights and mason jars as cups.

i panic when things change; heart inside lungs, fingernails in palms,
skin on fire. and as i've grown older, even my parents feel less
familiar, less like home. i panicked when i couldn't be there for my
sister's tenth birthday, the first one i've ever missed. i panic when i
think about how very soon i'll have to leave this place—these people,
these mountains—that've become so comfortable. how can i bring
myself to leave something that's nearly "good enough"? i panic when
i think about how i might never be able to stay put.
and then i realized, in the middle of a walmart parking lot, of all
places—

written all over my flesh,

"you are home,
you are home,
you are home."
these bones, this heart; i am my own home.

i could sail across the ocean, or get stuck in the middle of it, but i'll never be lost.

i am home.

tokyo

you must keep falling in love
knowing that it will destroy you

if you believe that this—romantic love,
infatuation,
obsession—will set you free
you will forever be
trapped in cages
you put yourself in

let it hurt
and bleed
and grow
and know that it is
not meant to be everything
you want,

yet,
it is everything
it is everything.

please, please, please

ears ringing
reminiscing
the simplicity of 16
nostalgic for the innocence
and naïve optimism
i'd just discovered the smiths
and the allure of twisted souls
the possibility of it all
of connection
of becoming
of leaving a speck
in the eye of a world
that didn't see me,
not yet

i could be anything.

lover, rescuer

a painful silence,
dragging on of snoozed alarms
set for no meetings

you will feel a slight
pressure to be better, to
feel alive again

and it is all up
to you; you must be your own
lover, rescuer

dryer sheets

i hope you know
that when i tell you goodnight
it's simply because
i love you
and not because
i need you

attach

i have become exactly what neither one of us wanted me to be—
believing i am incomplete without you.

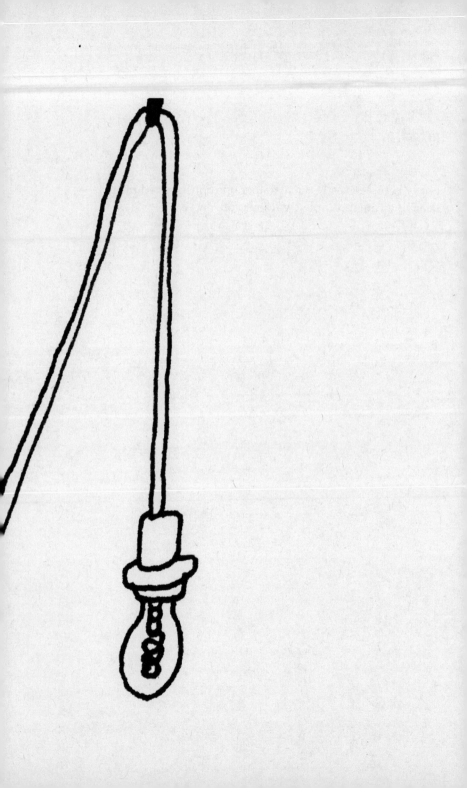

commit

i don't just want him to love me
i want him to choose me
over
and
over
again

i want him to see a light in me—*although it may flicker*

i want him to know,
i want him to be sure.

collapse

sometimes, i'm afraid that he treats me like a deranged housewife in circle skirt and plaid apron, holding a knife, waiting for him as he arrives home from work. he gently sets down his briefcase and reasons with me, slowly pulls away the kitchen aid and takes me into his arms where he can hold me in place until he feels i am less volatile, until he feels it is safe to be honest without such violent reactions, until he can gather up the children and take them to his mother's house, until he can safely tell me that he no longer wishes to stay.

piano songs

the sadness is so heavy
it sits on my chest, mimics the feeling
of standing in the middle of a blizzard in minnesota
i am so cold
i feel frozen
usually i cannot get my mind to seize scattered
thoughts
now, there is nothing
white, blank, open space
it is bitter
and empty
and numb
i cannot even indulge in the hurt
cannot cry along to sad songs or
find comfort in the vibrance of an open wound
it is all around me
yet,
there is nothing

liability

i feel so heavy
because i feel that
i am
so much
and i fear
letting anyone know
that i am not a feather
because boys like
simplicity
and i am anything
but that

boys don't settle down with
manic pixie dream girls,
they just kiss their necks
for a while
until they find someone
a little more boring
and a lot less burdensome

please don't go before i get better

september

i have lost myself so terribly,

but i'm starting to find a way back
slowly.

post-breakup treks

i went downtown to a show at a record store. the bands reminded me of bands i liked when i was fourteen, songs you played when you were my age. they screamed and played videos of puppies on a screen projector above them. i watched the shadows move back and forth and thought about you a lot, but i felt okay. i got my period in the bathroom and smiled. the sticker over the light switch said "you are beautiful." i thought the bassist was cute, but later i saw him with his girlfriend, who was the sister of the lead singer. they both wore glasses and matching flannels and smiled with their arms around one another. i thought they were probably perfect for each other. i thought they probably knew it.

the singer said, "this next one is a breakup song." at first it made me laugh and then i felt like i couldn't breathe. *i wish i wasn't a wreck since you left me. i wish i wasn't a wreck since you left me. i wish i wasn't a wreck since you left me.*

as i walked towards the back of the open room and out through the foggy glass doors, i wished i smoked so i had an excuse to sit outside on the sidewalk. i sat there anyway, up against the cold brick. my ears were ringing. i kept hoping someone would hit on me.

at ten o'clock, with black X's on the backs of my hands, i sat outside eating cheese puffs from the convenience store across the street. then i went home. but i didn't want to be alone, so i met a subaru outback in front of my house at midnight and left for a party full of people i didn't know.

we got there and i suddenly felt very small, like a child. i licked watermelon sugar off a lime-green baby bottle pop while everyone around me drank blue raspberry-flavored vodka and chain-smoked.

it was very amusing—both to them, and to me. a girl told me she heard what had happened, and that she was glad i was keeping busy. a boy named josh i'd never met before kept hugging me. he remembered my name, and was very happy for no reason at all.

and i stood in the middle of the hallway, listening to the voice of a stranger tell his friend about how he took photos of a girl kissing a boy who wasn't her boyfriend so she'd know what she did in the morning, and i thought about how nothing should hurt because we're all floating.

i undressed and fell into bed at three.

i didn't cry today, not once.

antidepressants

i think since i've gone on antidepressants, i've been perceived as cold (well, i know this—i've been told this) / which is a really strange thing for me to experience because i am a very warm and sensitive person / but the logical part of my brain has taken over, and i'm not used to functioning in a state of composure rather than intense emotion / i really don't think that i like it, i don't feel like me, i need to set up a doctor's appointment / but it has been really very nice not having so many panic attacks + feeling very happy for no reason at all.

the guilt of indifference

i've been listening to "make me dumb" by joyce manor on repeat all day because it makes my heart feel light. i have this driving loop i do when i feel like clearing my head and i screamed it with the windows down and i couldn't stop smiling. the weather was so beautiful today. i sat on my back porch and journaled. i ran errands in a dress and no coat. i felt so happy. this afternoon i cried for the first time in a while because i don't know why i feel the way i do (or why i seem to not feel anything at all), but only for a moment. all i really feel lately is indifference and happiness. i usually care so much about everything, usually feel so desperate or uneasy or empty. i don't really feel any of that anymore. i'm kind of just here . . . open and irrationally content. i met a boy in the dark last night past midnight at the playground. he smelled good and i liked the feeling of his fingers on my arm. i don't know if i was just tired or if all my emotions are dulled, but i didn't really know how to act. i didn't know how i felt. i feel like i cannot read myself at all anymore. like i'm a stranger even to myself. it's probably the medicine.

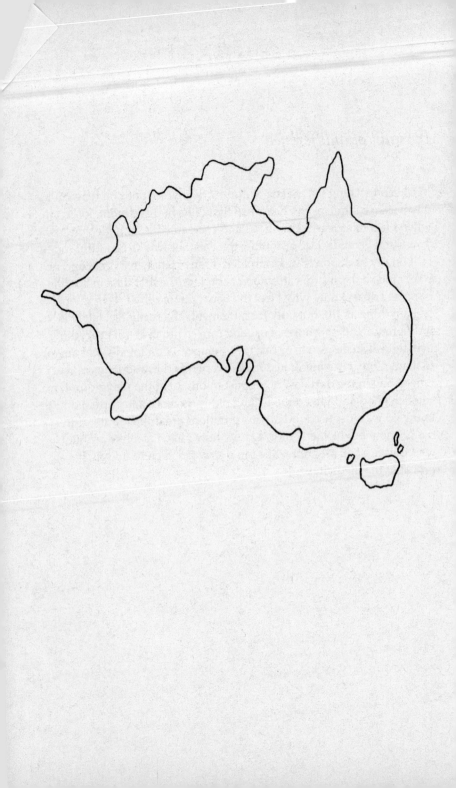

remember all the poems i wrote about him?

listening to a playlist an old "love" made for me. i'm thankful for all the connections i've had. i don't feel bitter, i don't feel longing. i look back on it fondly and feel warm, and grown, and i belly-laugh at my naïveté. my imagination and hopefulness is something i must always embrace. it is what i am best at—creating, romanticizing, embracing. i don't know him anymore, the boy i used to know, but i hope he is well. people can be chapters that you close forever without it being tragic. i can listen to old songs that remind me of him, and i don't miss him an ounce, but i wish for his happiness. how beautiful is that?

blue tang fish

obsessed with adoration
thirteen, sixteen
selfish and self-obsessed
his wife is making dinner in the kitchen while he
daydreams about my lips
another woman is thinking of me during a first date
with someone else

but i don't really care about them
only late at night, after independent films
highlighted forbidden infatuation
but it's not real,
not something i really want

in the end
i am repulsed,
repulsive

to those who believe that love isn't real

love is real, it's just not what we want it to be. i don't know if this idealized version of pure love exists. the only people i've ever loved selflessly are my siblings. i would do anything for them, not for any other reason except that they are special to me, and i want them to feel whole and happy—i want to give them everything i wish i'd had. i want to see them flourish. i want them to know that they are loved. my love for them is not based on how they treat me. they are children. their imperfections are expected. but romantic love is different. we're all fucked-up human beings with our own flaws and baggage, but we were taught by movies and books and songs that romantic love is the epitome of contentment . . . and it just isn't. not to me. love is real, but it isn't perfect. it's messy. and raw. and exhausting. relationships are hard. being fully vulnerable with someone who could leave at any moment takes a lot of courage. your siblings will never "leave" you. even as you grow up and spread out, they're just a phone call away. your parents will always be there (or at least that's supposed to be the agreement—but parents are fucked-up humans too). loving someone and accepting them for who they are, but still wanting to see them grow, takes a whole lot of compassion and patience. choosing someone again and again requires so much loyalty and commitment. romantic love seems to be the most intense form of intimacy. your partner affects you in ways that your platonic best friend or sister doesn't. i don't know. it's all so complicated. i think the moment we stop expecting romantic love to be something it's not is the moment it all feels okay. embrace the mess. embrace the chaos of being in love. you will learn that your love story is complex, or maybe it feels very simple. it hurts sometimes, it's fucking beautiful, and it's hard, and it's magic, and it's yours. it's all yours.

LOS ANGELES

los angeles

i am melting in the living room
of a house below the hills
while my boyfriend makes music with his friends,
i can hear it pulsing through the walls
as i read on their couch
bukowski screams that i am unoriginal,
rumi whispers that i am a part of something more;
we walk to the diner down the street
where the waitresses have stick-on gems beneath their
eyebrows
and choppy bleach-blond fringe entangled in their
eyelashes
and we are sitting at the counter at 10 p.m.
on top of red vinyl stools
drinking milkshakes and laughing and
not caring about anything
besides one another
and i am
arms outstretched through the sunroof
first day of summer
dancing in a sea of people to your favorite band
waking up on a sunday morning with him
happy

two months

i moved to california. i got on a plane at seven in the morning to fly over mountains and waters and fields of orange flowers i may never lie among. i cried in the car on the way there, trembling with fear and disbelief in myself. i looked out the window, thousands and thousands of feet above my safe spaces, and i smiled. i laughed. i marveled at the clouds.

every day, i get to look at palm trees and look in the mirror to see new freckles that have bloomed on my cheeks. i get to look back at the reflection of a girl who took a chance, a leap of faith, trusted her heart to guide her and believed that the universe would never hurt her without purpose. i look at someone who was afraid, stagnant, dead in a spiritual sense, but chose to see that there was more out there for her.

i walk everywhere. the sun tans my skin and i breathe in the smell of marijuana and flowers and i smile. i get up in the morning and i wash my face and i do yoga and i meditate. i sit in public places where i feel vulnerable and alone, and i let the panic pass instead of rushing home, and then i stay out for hours, soaking up the buzzing feeling of a holy-shit-i-really-am-getting-better high.

i am sitting on my couch in my apartment, my best friend (dog) next to me, sipping sleepytime tea while my beautiful boyfriend sleeps in our bed in the other room. i still have fear that growls in my stomach—i am learning not to feed myself to it anymore. i moved to california despite all his friends saying i shouldn't. and we are happy. and i love him. and i hope you get on a plane sometime soon, too.

move slowly

the world looks so different
smells
different
feels
different
when you move
slowly
watch your feet
take two steps inside of
a cement square
lift up one foot
and let it fall down like honey

i saw a hummingbird
for the first time
watched the wind blow through the palm trees
felt it on my face
smelled the purple flowers
on the sidewalk
didn't think about anything
at all besides
here
and
now
and
slowly,

slowly,

slow

neglect

i always wanted freckles on my lips
thought they were pretty
the way they were sprinkled
across her mouth
i wanted to be pretty too
wanted to look alive
feel alive
but i sat inside
running my tongue across my teeth
feeling the plaque and bits of spinach
stuck in between
and i didn't floss at night
i felt dizzy and breathless
lying on the carpeted floor
a fridge full of cold water
on the other side of the wall
i didn't move
i dripped in sweat and bathed in tears
red sand sitting between my rosy cheeks
if only i weren't so thirsty

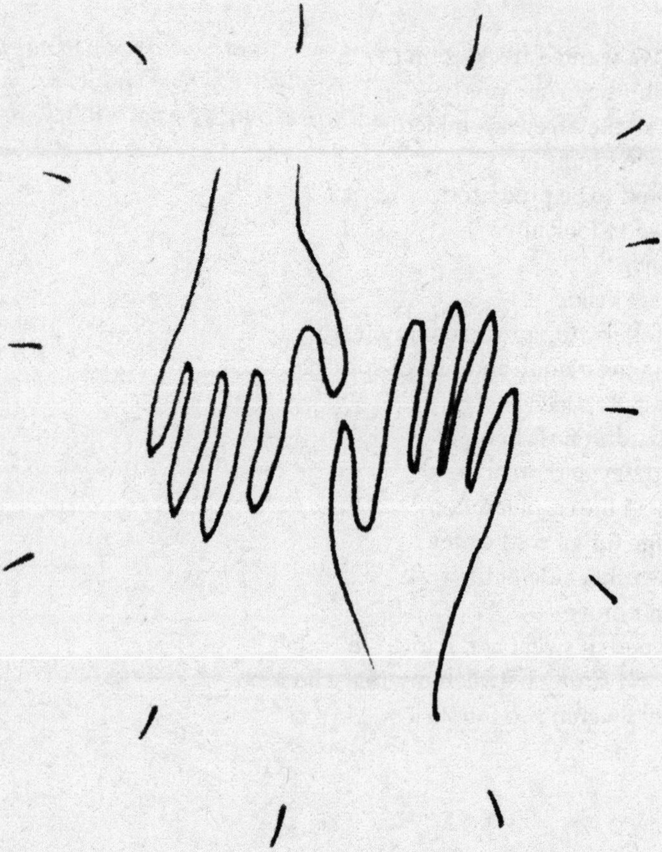

shoshana

i will beg the universe to never let me forget how it feels to be young
and with deepened smile lines and darkly freckled shoulders
my wrinkled, old, and worn hands grasping yours, i will try to
understand

i feel _lucky_ and _in love_
and _alive_ and _at peace_.
i wipe my feet on the welcome
mat, leave my muddy shoes
by the door, and fall into
a person who has
become my _home_.

kindling

he and i embodied ugliness for a long time. we fought habitually
and were venomous and resentful. life is different now. our love
is different now. the older we grow together, the more our hearts
soften. our stubborn, blind, selfish hearts learn to let go of being right
because mending and harmony are more important. i love him more
than my stubbornness now. when he pleads with me in frustration,
i don't stare at him with disgust like i used to and think about how i
need to escape. i try to understand. i see a man i love who is human
too. every day i feel closer to him. i feel proud of him. of both of us.
i feel lucky and in love and alive and at peace. i wipe my feet on the
welcome mat, leave my muddy shoes by the door, and fall into a
person who has become my home.

to my past muses

i wonder if you'll read the poems
i wrote about you
and what you'll think
if you'll care
roll your eyes
bite your lip
yawn
laugh
cry
i'll never fucking know

that's probably for the best

i'm not sure why i care what you think of me
i think i like knowing that i didn't
leave a bad taste in someone's mouth
i dream of you licking your lips
and tasting chamomile

you probably taste nothing at all

forgotten

intimate moments
of solitude
do not become memories
they are fleeting
rainbows caught in
midday sunlight
flowing in and out of
existence
i will not remember these moments,
painting my toenails on the front step
while my neighbor plays beach house
loudly through open windows
how the wind feels
how the aloneness feels
pure and new, yet familiar
how the contentment
the sureness
the mindfulness feels
like salty air sticking to your cheeks
on an afternoon at the beach
when you were little and nothing mattered
except for sand castles and sunscreen
i won't remember the time spent with only myself
my mind will crumble it up and toss it in the wash
like your favorite pair of socks
one never to be seen again
i won't remember
unless i write it down
because desert warmth
is somehow less significant
i don't think it should be

21

a cold bath takes the place
of a space designed for breathing slowly
her first glass of wine tastes like pretending
her favorite color is green
it sits on her lips like desperation, like apprehension
like maybe all of this tension will go away
if i try what i've seen my mother do a thousand times
she knows it won't work
but it feels okay. okay. okay.
okay. okay. okay.
i'm trying, i'm trying.

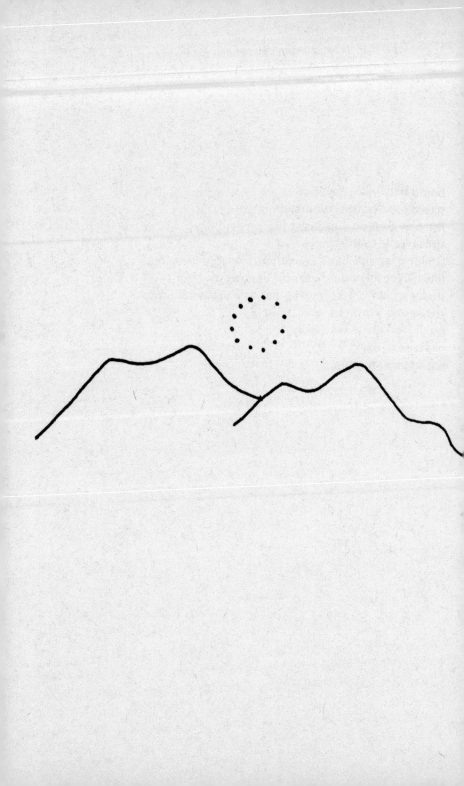

growing up

home is a tiny town and the blue ridge mountains
scenic trips down backroads with my sister,
listening to music while the wind makes our hair dance violently
sitting on my mom's back porch at sunset
late-night runs to dollar general
fifty-cent sodas from the machine outside of the grocery
store owned by the family of my best friend from the
sixth grade
watching my brother's baseball games at the park

but home is here, too.

the equinox

it feels like waking up

a dormant daffodil opening to
greet the warmth with ivory fervor

but it isn't spring, it's the end of summer
the sun has always been there

yet i hide inside the warm ground
amongst the worms and the rot
and pretend it's okay

until i get a glimpse of light
a gentle and burning ray of reminding

of what it's like to be open

coda

➤»————

i'm walking my dog; the littlest one. he has his nose to the ground and his black tail curled upwards. i pass a man on the sidewalk with strong arms and brown hair. i hate his clothes but i love his eyes. he looks at me like a television ad; no interest at all, just a blank stare. when i get to my building, i see you. you're tall and your hands are in your pockets. i'm not surprised at all. i always knew you were coming.

"there you are," i say.

you look at me with relief shimmering in your eyes. you didn't know what i'd do. you flew halfway across the world to stand in front of me and watch me walk away.

"here i am," you say.

i walk towards you slowly, like if i move too quickly, you'll blow away with the wind rustling the palm trees above us. i've dropped the leash and fin is running towards the busy street. when i'm close enough to smell the cologne clinging to your wrists, you tuck a piece of hair behind my ear. my heart slows instead of quickens. i feel calm. i feel seen. i feel you.

we step into my apartment and i've cleared my mind of anything else but you. all i can see is your tan skin and dark eyes. you sit down on the chair by the door.

you hold me like a child while my body convulses and tears dampen your shirt. i feel everything all at once.

you are here, and i am finally gone.

➤»————

my head is swirling

       spinning?

it's dizzy and messy and blind

i knew things had changed when
i didn't hear the door crack open
and see you standing there,
pillow in hand,
asking to join me on the couch

➤》────────

i sit on the sidewalk like a shiny penny
waiting to be picked up or for my glistening
to catch the eye of a stranger
but instead they are chattering and laughing
and completely silent
their shoes leaving black scuff marks on my surface
slowly dulling me into the pavement and
i realize i am not anything new
just another piece of loose change

>»————

this is the second night this week
that you've shown up while i sleep
i dreamt you were crying and i felt that we could love each
other better than my past love
because you understood what it was like to feel broken
to feel loss
to have endured true tragedy and found yourself
heaving under the weight of it all and
you weren't afraid to let me see you bawl and contort
you rested your forehead on my shoulder and
i knew we could love each other
because we understood

i've spent the day reading and writing and pretending i don't have anything better to do. it amazes me that my grandmother had such beautiful script and mine is just god-awful. i think even if i practiced it would still be hideous. i'm very good at admiring beautiful things and terrible at embodying them. i think i'm destined to be an onlooker while everyone else blooms and is adored. even if their words don't mean shit, they look pretty so they're a revelation. it's easy to seem wise and deep when you're regurgitating sayings and thoughts that have been thought and said for centuries. but they are oh so concise and convenient and easily digested. sometimes i find myself wishing i could be so simple, so contrived, just for the approval and esteem. i am so addicted to the idea of being revered. a universal infatuation. i value it over genuineness and reality and substance. why? why do i hope for an unreliable love that is lacking in so many other ways? it will not remind me to brush my teeth or drink water. it will only braid my hair and feed my ego until i am fat with it, and he has found someone new to "love."

i crave a lover who will write me poems

or at least one who will want to read mine.

➜»———

i think i'll move back home and
make a dozen boys fall in love with me just to prove to
myself that i am more than he made me feel i was
i've given myself to him for the past three years but i think
he wouldn't like me if he really got to know me
despite sharing a bed for so long
he doesn't really know me
not really

→))————

i am selfish when i am craving attention. affection. i won't care if you
have a girlfriend. i'll let you send me shirtless photos and pretend that
we're oblivious to the inappropriateness of it all. i will swallow my
morals and keep the ugly secret. you aren't flirting, you aren't getting
high off the idea that i am looking at you in your boxers with tattoos
across your chest and molten glass in your smile. you are just saying
hello. and i am just saying it back.

but when i find a place to put my love, i will fucking die for you.
i will hand over all my rations until you are fat and happy, and i am
shriveled and happy. i will follow you across the country and i will
take care of your dog and i will do your laundry. i will love you even
when you yell at me. i will try to kiss you when you turn away. i
will write poems and you won't read them. i will pretend that this is
enough. this is enough. this is enough. this is enough. this is enough.
this is—

but, jesus, he looks so good without a shirt on.

➤➤———

i don't burn bridges
i just let them rot
let the termites eat away at the timber
forget they're even there
until i return to my hometown
and it feels like a ghost town
no high school sweethearts to ring for coffee
no old study buddies to catch up with over gas station
sandwiches
no one to curl into with nostalgia
no rickety planks, no pile of ashes
just a muddy stream flowing through the green and brown
overgrowth
unaware that life exists apart from solitude

→»————

i used to read about how pisces are known for their self-sacrifice.
he convinced me that this did not apply to me. but as i sit here on
a sidewalk in west hollywood, thinking about how many times
i've filled my suitcases to follow him around—to philadelphia, to
sweaty florida, to hopeless delaware, to north carolina, to loss of self,
to here—i realize he was wrong. i sat on trains, buses, planes, and
drove miles and miles to give you my heart, even when you weren't
ready to give me yours. i gave up my own dreams to follow yours.
you tried to tell me i didn't have any, so what was the fuss for? but i
never dreamed of being this dependent, fearful person, swollen with
self-doubt. i never dreamed of having to look to you before making
a move. i never dreamed of being twenty-one and ready to give up
new york city, incense, and—. i didn't dream of losing myself. but
i did—i lost myself in giving myself and not knowing how to keep
enough intact. i know you'll read this (if you ever actually do) and
think i'm remembering you worse than you were. i don't resent you
or even really blame you. i'm just excited to dream again, instead of
pretending yours were mine, and that that was enough.

➤≫————

he has a tattoo below his elbow
of a bird, dedicated to his grandmother
and i want to make him cut his hair
run his fingers through mine
kiss me until my chin is red
make him forget about jesus
make him love me for a while

i'm afraid he thinks i am too good for him—
i wish he knew i am not good enough for anyone

➤»————

her heart stopped beating for a moment—
immediately after, she could not recall why;
perhaps it was the song playing faintly
in the corner of her dark room, a man
screaming, a soul singing of devotion

or maybe it was the thought of
the pennies in her bank account, copper stained
with evidence of impulse and manic depression

maybe it was the memory of saying hello
to an old boyfriend at the coffee bar today,
the one she pretended not to see in the hallway
when she was fifteen and terrified, and
again, this morning, five years later

still the same tangle of butterfly-wing veins
and self-doubt, a young girl
with messy hair and hollow stomach

or maybe it was the thought of him,
a boy like the fog that hovers in the mountains
between her hometown and the next one over;
someone she could get lost in

—maybe it was you.

➤»——————

i hate feeling like this
like i'm some unworthy person because i can't believe the things you do
like that small girl in middle school, surrounded by laughing faces
of course, he'd never go for you

because i am a nonbeliever
i am sin
i am covered in it
and when i take my last breath
i will smile, thinking about the beautiful life i've lived
the things i've seen, the people i've loved, the art i've shared
how i tried so hard to be good

all the air will leave my lungs
and with my eyes closed,
grin still there,
you will cover me with leaves
you will set me on the water
and say goodbye as i sail into flames
this is where you believe i belong
you believe this
you do

➤⟫————

a memory that will not be tarnished by the reality of an abandoned
love—
i think the most alive i ever felt was when he kissed me in the
doorway of that cramped restaurant in chinatown. we were blocking
the entryway, a knot of puffer coats and scarves, as he stuck his
tongue inside my mouth. a group of middle-aged couples rolled their
eyes and waited impatiently to push past us. he didn't care. i was
embarrassed but too enthralled and engulfed to let it bother me. we
laughed as we tumbled out into the twilight. my hands were frozen but i
held his out in the cold air anyway. we were not looking backwards or
forwards, just down at our feet on the philadelphia sidewalk.

as expected, the electricity has gone out; we forgot to pay the bill. two
lovers wandering in the dark, unaware of warm cheeks neglected.

and now i am left questioning what it takes to keep the lights on.

➤»————

there are three record stores in town
i'm going to visit all of them in hopes
you'll be behind the counter when i walk through the door
i'll look straight at you, hold it, let there be no mistake
that we've acknowledged each other's existence
your green eyes, my grey scarf
we are here, now, real
then i'll look away
flip through the albums, halfheartedly searching for new order or
fleetwood mac
decide that i'm bored
and leave

i'll pretend that you care
you won't in the slightest

➤»————

i cannot sleep
it tastes like blood in my mouth
do you bite the insides of your cheeks like me?
pick at your blisters like me?
are you unable to let anything heal without a little scarring?
do you make a home in the open wounds?
there they are. they are there. they've always been there.
are we the same?
are we the same?
are we?
are we?
are we?

➤»————

after reading forty pages of romantic nineteenth-century literature, i've decided that getting my feelings hurt is not the end of the world. i'd like to know you. just you and i, apart from anything. i hope you know that the idea of you—and what i know of the actual you thus far—excites me, and considering you as a muse is inevitable. reference of you is bound to end up in my messy streams of consciousness. you seem like someone who'd be a mistake to disregard. i'm afraid you'll wake up to this and deem me insane for giving so much thought to someone i hardly know. it's possible i am. i'm sure i'll dream of you. goodnight, again.

➤»———

perhaps it is the pills—
at the surface and deep down
i really hope it is

i am so accustomed to
stomach drops and aching chests
i don't know what to do with feeling
like the world is not ending
like i have hope in all outcomes
like i can flip a coin and walk away
before it hits the ground

maybe this is what security feels like
maybe i won't always feel everything in extremes

maybe i can write poetry
close my journal
turn the lights out
roll over
and fall asleep

➤»————

maybe one day we will return to one another
we will share stories of our time apart
and fall asleep in the same bed again

and we will be happy.

and maybe one day we will find love apart—
you and your fierce love, who wears braids in her hair
and will talk to you until dawn;
you won't be able to get her to shut up
me and my gentle love, who brings me flowers
and likes the way i dress;
a love that burns and a love that heals

and we will be happy.

afterword

let me begin with this: sometimes you must go through things, totally and completely, to fully understand them.

the past few years of my life were a whirlwind. i saw myself as broken, and i didn't know how to fix things. or maybe i did, but i didn't know how to muster up the courage to do so. i crossed my arms and furrowed my brow and screamed while keeping my feet planted firmly on the ground. then, one day, i decided to move. i woke up and realized that i would rather be lost and broken down on the side of the road without a phone than sink deeper and deeper into a foam pit of comfort and lethargy. i wanted to feel alive again.

for weeks, i'd stay up late at night looking at flights online, picking at my cuticles and replaying a scene in my head over and over again of me navigating the airport until finally, i bought a one-way ticket that would set me free. moving across the country was the best decision i ever made. it was an awakening. i look back and realize i had to be fully immersed in all of that darkness to really understand it and myself.

on those overexposed and oversaturated months in los angeles, i'd wake up in the morning and walk my dog—some days taking a quick loop around the block, other days not worrying how far away from home we wandered. i did yoga in my living room and told myself i was more capable than i realized. i entered anxious situations and reminded myself that not trying is more harmful than doing the thing that scares me. there are still things i want that i do not have yet. i have so much more to learn. i'll always be learning. life is a constant torrent of trying to figure shit out and doing your best.

in october, i purchased another one-way ticket. i left a love that grew me and shaped me but did not nourish me in the ways that my soul ached for. i said goodbye to açaí bowls and palm trees, and kissed my best friend of three years goodbye. some might feel that traveling across the country for a relationship that would end was just a waste of time. an immature and starry-eyed adolescent mistake—but i don't see it that way. i look in the mirror and i see someone brave. someone full of hope, someone who chose to chase warmth all while knowing the real possibility of imperfect endings. i believe that fairy tales don't always end in happily ever after. mine ended in tears and poorly taped cardboard boxes—but it was still magic. i will forever cherish the time i spent with the person who so many of these poems are about. he was a temporary home, one that i'll go out of my way to drive by every so often, giggling at the new garden gnomes and christmas decorations put up by the latest occupant.

we are so lucky to love, to know the light and dark parts of each other's souls, to get to feel anything at all. none of it is in vain. we turn the hurt into art, into poetry, into stories to share that create unity in understanding. the bliss turns into polaroids we tape above our desks, montages we play back in our minds set to blaring eighties european rock.

i used to see the stages of my life only as steps towards improvement. i thought i had to justify everything with my desire to be better; seeing present sorrow as a fleeting phase. like somehow, the lulls of depression and anxiety, the slower days, the dull minutes were not me. but they are. every moment is valid. every moment counts. and we must learn to love who we are right now, apart from who we could be in the future. we are more than just the highlight reel. we are the moments in between. the messy hair and the drunken irrationalities. we should find peace in the lazy afternoons, instead of criticizing the inactivity. learn what drains you and what makes you whole. focus on the here and the now and the good. you are here, you are now, and you are good.

i used to fear abandonment because i thought that my imperfections made me inferior. that to earn the affection of someone i cared for, i had to beg them, *please don't go before i get better.* i believed that someday i would reach this ideal version of myself and suddenly everything would fall into place and i'd ride off into an endless sunset of well-being and stability. and then i discovered that my imperfections do not make me lesser, they just make me human. and these flaws are not detached or impersonal, they are essential notes in the composition of my depth. and unrealistic sunsets should not be the motivation, but rather, the beauty of all that imperfection. the gift of feeling. the luck of existing.

and the chance to write poetry about it all.

acknowledgments

I am a product of all those who have supported and believed in me. Thank you to my agents, Erin Harris and Katherine Latshaw, for seeking me out and having a vision for this collection, one so much larger than I had imagined. To my editor, Natasha Simons, for your passion for bringing my words to so many more souls.

Thank you, Leah Lu, for being a friend and a brilliant artist. I am so glad we found each other on social media when we were teenagers, and through serendipitous magic, teamed up for this book and laughed together in my living room in West Hollywood. I am so excited to see where your creativity and honesty take you.

To my mother, whose unceasing encouragement has kept me afloat, even in the darkest moments. Thank you for always being there to instill hope in me. To Natalie and Jake, my favorite people in the whole world—thank you for making me a big sister. Thank you for the snuggles and the belly laughs and acceptance.

To Aunt Judy, for the hour-long phone calls full of comfort and wisdom. Thank you for always motivating me to live in gratitude, to take each moment as it comes, and to value compassion and kindness above everything. I love you like a mother and, like everyone who knows you, feel blessed by your existence.

To my muses, especially Christopher. Thank you, C., for being my best friend. Thank you for helping me grow, motivating me to see through different lenses, and teaching me how to build IKEA furniture on my own. You've changed me forever, and I will always carry you in my heart.

To my readers, my followers, my soul mates. Putting my appreciation into words is difficult. I wish I could just give you a bear hug instead. Thank you for understanding the messiest parts of me, and for reminding me that I have a friend wherever I go.